FIRST CUP DEVOTIONS

FOR
MEN

The quoted ideas expressed in this book (but not scripture verses) are not, in all cases, exact quotations, as some have been edited for clarity and brevity. In all cases, the author has attempted to maintain the speaker's original intent. In some cases, quoted material for this book was obtained from secondary sources, primarily print media. While every effort was made to ensure the accuracy of these sources, the accuracy cannot be guaranteed. For additions, deletions, corrections or clarifications in future editions of this text, please write FAMILY CHRISTIAN PRESS.

Scripture quotations are taken from:

The Holy Bible, King James Version

The Holy Bible, New International Version (NIV) Copyright © 1973, 1978, 1984, by International Bible Society. Used by permission of Zondervan Publishing House. All rights reserved.

The Holy Bible, New King James Version (NKJV) Copyright © 1982 by Thomas Nelson, Inc. Used by permission.

The New American Standard Bible®, (NASB) Copyright © 1960, 1962, 1963, 1968, 1971, 1972, 1973, 1975, 1977, 1995 by The Lockman Foundation. Used by permission.

Holy Bible, New Living Translation, (NLT)copyright © 1996. Used by permission of Tyndale House Publishers, Inc., Wheaton, Illinois 60189. All rights reserved.

The Message (MSG)- This edition issued by contractual arrangement with NavPress, a division of The Navigators, U.S.A. Originally published by NavPress in English as THE MESSAGE: The Bible in Contemporary Language copyright 2002-2003 by Eugene Peterson. All rights reserved.

New Century Version®. (NCV) Copyright © 1987, 1988, 1991 by Word Publishing, a division of Thomas Nelson, Inc. All rights reserved. Used by permission.

The Holman Christian Standard Bible™ (HCSB) Copyright © 1999, 2000, 2001 by Holman Bible Publishers. Used by permission.

Cover Design by Kim Russell / Wahoo Designs
Page Layout by Bart Dawson

ISBN 1-58334-273-7

Printed in the United States of America

FIRST CUP
DEVOTIONS

FOR
MEN

TABLE OF CONTENTS

Introduction: First Things First   9

Day 1 It All Starts with God   11

Day 2 This Is the Day   15

Day 3 What Will Your Attitude Be Today?   19

Day 4 The Words You Speak Today   23

Day 5 The Time for Obedience   27

Day 6 Living Courageously   31

Day 7 Priorities That Are Pleasing to God   35

Day 8 Whom Will You Encourage Today?   39

Day 9 A Humble Heart   43

Day 10 When the Day Is Difficult   47

Day 11 Encountering God in the Here and Now   51

Day 12 Wisdom for Today   55

Day 13 The Power of Perseverance   59

Day 14 A Day Filled with Laugher   63

Day 15 How Will You Lead?   67

Day 16 The Opportunity to Forgive   71

Day 17 And the Greatest of These . . .   75

Day 18 Genuine Peace   79

Day 19 The Temptations of Everyday Life   83

Day 20 Making the Most of Your Talents Today   87

Day 21 Happiness Now   91

Day 22 A Day Filled with Prayer   95

Day 23 The Power of Purpose   99

Day 24 What Kind of Example
          Will You Be Today?   103

Day 25 The Magic of the Morning   107

Day 26 Whom Will You Serve Today?   111

Day 27 The Path to Spiritual Growth   115

Day 28 Taking Time to Give Thanks   119

Day 29 Receiving God's Abundance   123

Day 30 Accepting God's Gift   127

Bible Verses to Consider   131

INTRODUCTION:
FIRST THINGS FIRST

How do you begin your day? Do you awaken early enough to enjoy that first cup of hot coffee while studying your Bible and spending at least a few quiet moments with God? Or are you one of those men who sleep until the last possible minute, leaving no time to invest in matters of the heart and soul? Hopefully, you make a habit of spending precious moments each morning with your Creator. When you do, He will fill your heart, He will direct your thoughts, and He will guide your steps.

Daily life is woven together with the threads of habit, and no habit is more important to your spiritual growth than the discipline of daily prayer and devotion to God.

This book contains devotional readings that are intended to set the tone for the rest of your day. The text is divided into 30 chapters, one for each day of the month. Each chapter contains Bible verses, quotations, brief essays, and prayers, all of which can help you focus your thoughts on the countless blessings and opportunities that God has placed before you.

During the next 30 days, please try this experiment: Read one chapter each morning with your first cup of coffee. If you're already committed to a daily worship time, this book will enrich that experience. If you are not, the simple act of giving God a few minutes each morning will change the tone and direction of your life.

Your daily devotional time can be habit-forming, and should be. The first few minutes of each day are invaluable. Treat them that way, and offer them to God.

IT ALL STARTS WITH GOD

JESUS SAID TO HIM,
"YOU SHALL LOVE THE LORD YOUR GOD
WITH ALL YOUR HEART, WITH ALL YOUR SOUL,
AND WITH ALL YOUR MIND."
THIS IS THE FIRST AND GREAT COMMANDMENT.

MATTHEW 22:37-38 NKJV

C. S. Lewis observed, "A man's spiritual health is exactly proportional to his love for God." If we are to enjoy the spiritual health that God intends for us, we must praise Him, we must love Him, and we must obey Him.

When we worship God faithfully and obediently, we invite His love into our hearts. When we truly worship God, we allow Him to rule over our days and our lives. In turn, we grow to love God even more deeply as we sense His love for us.

St. Augustine wrote, "I love you, Lord, not doubtingly, but with absolute certainty. Your Word beat upon my heart until I fell in love with you, and now the universe and everything in it tells me to love you."

This morning, as you make plans for the day ahead, open your heart to the Father. And let your obedience be a fitting response to His never-ending love.

The only way to love God with all our soul
is to give up our lives for His sake.

OSWALD CHAMBERS

Telling the Lord how much you love Him and
why is what praise and worship are all about.

LISA WHELCHEL

Christians have spent their whole lives
mastering all sorts of principles, done their duty,
carried on the programs of their church . . .
and never known God intimately, heart to heart.

JOHN ELDREDGE

The only true source of meaning in life is found
in love for God and his son Jesus Christ,
and love for mankind,
beginning with our own families.

JAMES DOBSON

MORE FROM GOD'S WORD

And he has given us this command:
Whoever loves God must also love his brother.

1 JOHN 4:21 NIV

I will sing of the LORD's great love forever;
with my mouth I will make your faithfulness
known through all generations.

PSALM 89:1 NIV

TODAY, I WILL THINK ABOUT . . .

Ways that I can honor God by
placing Him first in my life.

A PRAYER TO START MY DAY

Dear Heavenly Father, You have blessed me with
a love that is infinite and eternal. Let me love You,
Lord, more and more each day. Make me a loving
servant, Father, today and throughout eternity.
And, let me show my love for You by sharing
Your message and Your love with others. —Amen

THIS IS THE DAY

THIS IS THE DAY THE LORD HAS MADE;

WE WILL REJOICE AND BE GLAD IN IT.

PSALM 118:24 NKJV

What do you expect from the day ahead? Are you expecting God to do wonderful things, or are you living beneath a cloud of apprehension and doubt? The familiar words of Psalm 118:24 remind us of a profound yet simple truth: God made this day and gave it to us as a gift. We, in response to that gift, should be grateful.

For Christian believers, every day begins and ends with God and His Son. Christ came to this earth to give us abundant life and eternal salvation. We give thanks to our Maker when we treasure each day and use it to the fullest.

Today, let us give thanks for the gift of life and for the One who created it. And then, let's use this day—a precious gift from the Father above—to serve our Savior faithfully, courageously, and joyfully.

Now is the only time worth having because,
indeed, it is the only time we have.

C. H. SPURGEON

With each new dawn, life delivers a package
to your front door, rings your doorbell, and runs.

CHARLES SWINDOLL

Today is mine. Tomorrow is none of my business.
If I peer anxiously into the fog of the future,
I will strain my spiritual eyes so that
I will not see clearly what is required of me now.

ELISABETH ELLIOT

Wherever you are, be all there.
Live to the hilt every situation you believe
to be the will of God.

JIM ELLIOT

Every day should be a fantastic adventure for us
because we're in the middle of God's
unfolding plan for the ages.

JOHN MACARTHUR

MORE FROM GOD'S WORD

*So don't worry about tomorrow,
for tomorrow will bring its own worries.
Today's trouble is enough for today.*

MATTHEW 6:34 NLT

Encourage one another daily, as long as it is Today . . . .

HEBREWS 3:13 NIV

TODAY, I WILL THINK ABOUT . . .

The importance of living in the present moment
and the importance of celebrating
the present moment.

A PRAYER TO START MY DAY

Help me, Father, to learn from the past but not
live in it. And, help me to plan for the future
but not to worry about it. This is the day that You
have given me, Lord. Let me use it according to
Your master plan, and let me give thanks for
Your blessings. Enable me to live each moment to
the fullest, totally involved in Your will. —Amen

WHAT WILL YOUR ATTITUDE BE TODAY?

FINALLY BROTHERS, WHATEVER IS TRUE,
WHATEVER IS HONORABLE, WHATEVER IS JUST,
WHATEVER IS PURE, WHATEVER IS LOVELY,
WHATEVER IS COMMENDABLE—IF THERE IS
ANY MORAL EXCELLENCE AND IF THERE IS
ANY PRAISE—DWELL ON THESE THINGS.

PHILIPPIANS 4:8 HCSB

As you make plans for the upcoming day, here's a question: How will you direct your thoughts today? Will you obey the words of Philippians 4:8 by dwelling upon those things that are honorable, true, and worthy of praise? Or will you allow your thoughts to be hijacked by the negativity that seems to dominate our troubled world?

Are you fearful, angry, bored, or worried? Are you so preoccupied with the concerns of this day that you fail to thank God for the promise of eternity? Are you confused, bitter, or pessimistic? If so, God wants to have a little talk with you.

God intends that you experience joy and abundance, but He will not force His joy upon you; you must claim it for yourself. So, today and every day hereafter, celebrate this life that God has given you by focusing your thoughts and your energies upon "whatever is of good repute." Today, count your blessings instead of your hardships. And thank the Giver of all things good for gifts that are simply too numerous to count.

The way you see life will largely determine
what you get out of it.

ZIG ZIGLAR

Outlook determines outcome and
attitude determines action.

WARREN WIERSBE

Whenever a negative thought concerning
your personal power comes to mind, deliberately
voice a positive thought to cancel it out.

NORMAN VINCENT PEALE

The things we think are the things that feed
our souls. If we think on pure and lovely things, we
shall grow pure and lovely like them;
and the converse is equally true.

HANNAH WHITALL SMITH

You've heard the saying, "Life is what you make it."
That means we have a choice. We can choose
to have a life full of frustration and fear, but we can
just as easily choose one of joy and contentment.

DENNIS SWANBERG

MORE FROM GOD'S WORD

For God has not given us a spirit of fear,
but of power and of love and of a sound mind.

2 TIMOTHY 1:7 NLT

All the days of the oppressed are wretched,
but the cheerful heart has a continual feast.

PROVERBS 15:15 NIV

TODAY, I WILL THINK ABOUT . . .

The power of positive thinking and the cost of
negative thinking.

A PRAYER TO START MY DAY

Lord, I pray for an attitude that is Christlike.
Whatever my situation, whether good or bad, happy
or sad, let me respond with an attitude of optimism,
faith, and love for You. —Amen

THE WORDS YOU SPEAK TODAY

> RASH LANGUAGE CUTS AND MAIMS,
> BUT THERE IS HEALING IN
> THE WORDS OF THE WISE.
>
> PROVERBS 12:18 MSG

Think . . . pause . . . then speak: How wise is the man who can communicate in this way. But all too often, in the rush to have ourselves heard, we speak first and think next . . . with unfortunate results.

God's Word reminds us that "Reckless words pierce like a sword, but the tongue of the wise brings healing" (Proverbs 12:18 NIV). If we seek to be a source of encouragement to friends and family, then we must measure our words carefully. Words are important: they can hurt or heal. Words can uplift us or discourage us, and reckless words, spoken in haste, cannot be erased.

Today, seek to encourage all who cross your path. Measure your words carefully. Speak wisely, not impulsively. Use words of kindness and praise, not words of anger or derision. Remember that you have the power to heal others or to injure them, to lift others up or to hold them back. When you lift them up, your wisdom will bring healing and comfort to a world that needs both.

Attitude and the spirit in which we communicate
are as important as the words we say.

CHARLES STANLEY

A little kindly advice is better
than a great deal of scolding.

FANNY CROSBY

I still believe we ought to talk about Jesus.
The old country doctor of my boyhood days
always began his examination by saying,
"Let me see your tongue." That's a good way
to check a Christian: the tongue test.
Let's hear what he is talking about.

VANCE HAVNER

The battle of the tongue is won not in the mouth,
but in the heart.

ANNIE CHAPMAN

When you talk, choose the very same words
that you would use if Jesus were looking
over your shoulder. Because He is.

MARIE T. FREEMAN

MORE FROM GOD'S WORD

May the words of my mouth and the thoughts
of my heart be pleasing to you, O LORD,
my rock and my redeemer.

PSALM 19:14 NLT

Out of the abundance of the heart the mouth speaks.

MATTHEW 12:34 NKJV

TODAY, I WILL THINK ABOUT . . .

The importance of measuring my words carefully,
especially when I'm frustrated, tired, or angry.

A PRAYER TO START MY DAY

Lord, You have warned me that I will be judged by
the words I speak. And, You have commanded me
to choose my words carefully so that I might be
a source of encouragement and hope to all whom
I meet. Keep me mindful, Lord, that I have influence
on many people . . . make me an influence for good.
And may the words that I speak today be worthy of
the One who has saved me forever. —Amen

THE TIME
FOR
OBEDIENCE

JESUS ANSWERED, "IF ANYONE LOVES ME,
HE WILL KEEP MY WORD.
MY FATHER WILL LOVE HIM,
AND WE WILL COME TO HIM AND
MAKE OUR HOME WITH HIM."

JOHN 14:23 HCSB

Obedience to God is determined, not by words, but by deeds. Talking about righteousness is easy; living righteously is far more difficult, especially in today's temptation-filled world.

Since God created Adam and Eve, we human beings have been rebelling against our Creator. Why? Because we are unwilling to trust God's Word, and we are unwilling to follow His commandments. God has given us a guidebook for righteous living called the Holy Bible. It contains thorough instructions which, if followed, lead to fulfillment, righteousness and salvation. But, if we choose to ignore Gods commandments, the results are as predictable as they are tragic.

Unless we are willing to abide by God's laws, all of our righteous proclamations ring hollow. How can we best proclaim our love for the Lord? By obeying Him. And, for further instructions, read the manual.

If you want to discover your spiritual gifts,
start obeying God. As you serve Him,
you will find that He has given you the gifts
that are necessary to follow through in obedience.

ANNE GRAHAM LOTZ

Let me tell you—there is no "high"
like the elation and joy that come from
a sacrificial act of obedience.

BILL HYBELS

Only he who believes is obedient,
and only he who is obedient believes.

DIETRICH BONHOEFFER

There is sharp necessity for giving Christ
absolute obedience. The devil bids for our complete
self-will. To whatever extent we give this self-will
the right to be master over our lives, we are,
to an extent, giving Satan a toehold.

CATHERINE MARSHALL

MORE FROM GOD'S WORD

Blessed is every one who fears the LORD,
who walks in His ways.

PSALM 128:1 NKJV

For God is working in you, giving you the desire
to obey him and the power to do what pleases him.

PHILIPPIANS 2:13 NLT

TODAY, I WILL THINK ABOUT . . .

The blessings that I receive when
I obey God's commandments.

A PRAYER TO START MY DAY

Dear Heavenly Father, You have blessed me
with a love that is infinite and eternal. Let me
demonstrate my love for You by obeying Your
commandments. Make me a faithful servant, Father,
today and throughout eternity. And, let me show
my love for You by sharing Your message and
Your love with others. —Amen

LIVING COURAGEOUSLY

THE LORD IS THE ONE WHO WILL
GO BEFORE YOU. HE WILL BE WITH YOU;
HE WILL NOT LEAVE YOU OR FORSAKE YOU.
DO NOT BE AFRAID OR DISCOURAGED.

DEUTERONOMY 31:8 HCSB

Every human life is a tapestry of events: some grand, some not so grand, and some downright disheartening. When we reach the mountaintops of life, praising God is easy. In our moments of triumph, we trust God's plan. But, when the storm clouds form overhead and we find ourselves in the dark valley of despair, our faith is stretched, sometimes to the breaking point. As Christians, we can be comforted: Wherever we find ourselves, whether at the top of the mountain or the depths of the valley, God is there, and because He cares for us, we can live courageously.

Christians have every reason to be courageous. After all, the ultimate battle has already been fought and won on the cross at Calvary. But, even dedicated followers of Christ may find their courage tested by the inevitable disappointments and tragedies that occur in the lives of believers and non-believers alike.

Sometime today, your courage may be tested to the limit. When you are tested, remember that God is as near as your next breath, and remember that He offers salvation to His children. He is your shield and your strength; He is your protector and your deliverer. Call upon Him in your hour of need and then be comforted. Whatever your challenge, whatever your trouble, God can handle it. And will.

If a person fears God, he or she has no reason to fear
anything else. On the other hand, if a person
does not fear God, then fear becomes a way of life.

BETH MOORE

Courage is not simply one of the virtues,
but the form of every virtue at the testing point,
which means, at the point of highest reality.
A chastity or honesty or mercy which yields to
danger will be chaste or honest or merciful
only on conditions. Pilate was merciful
till it became risky.

C. S. LEWIS

Courage is almost a contradiction in terms.
It means a strong desire to live
taking the form of a readiness to die.

G. K. CHESTERTON

Dreaming the dream of God is not for cowards.

JOEY JOHNSON

MORE FROM GOD'S WORD

Be strong and courageous, and do the work.
Do not be afraid or discouraged,
for the LORD God, my God, is with you.

1 CHRONICLES 28:20 NIV

Therefore, being always of good courage . . .
we walk by faith, not by sight.

2 CORINTHIANS 5:6-7 NASB

TODAY, I WILL THINK ABOUT . . .
The rewards of living courageously.

A PRAYER TO START MY DAY

Dear Lord, sometimes I face disappointments and
challenges that leave me worried and afraid.
When I am fearful, let me seek Your strength.
When I am anxious, give me faith.
Keep me mindful, Lord, that You are my God.
With You by my side, Lord, I have nothing to fear.
Help me to be Your grateful and courageous servant
this day and every day. —Amen

PRIORITIES THAT ARE PLEASING TO GOD

THE THING YOU SHOULD WANT MOST IS
GOD'S KINGDOM AND DOING WHAT GOD WANTS.
THEN ALL THESE OTHER THINGS
YOU NEED WILL BE GIVEN TO YOU.

MATTHEW 6:33 NCV

As you think about the day ahead, you're probably hoping that you can accomplish "first things first." But, as a busy man living in a demanding world, you understand that placing first things first can be difficult indeed. Why? Because so many people are expecting so many things from you!

If you're having trouble prioritizing your day, perhaps you've been trying to organize your life according to your own plans, not God's. A better strategy, of course, is to take your daily obligations and place them in the hands of the One who created you. To do so, you must prioritize your day according to God's commandments, and you must seek His will and His wisdom in all matters. Then, you can face the day with the assurance that the same God who created our universe out of nothingness will help you place first things first in your own life.

Do you feel overwhelmed or confused? Turn the concerns of this day over to God—prayerfully, earnestly, and often. Then, listen for His answer . . . and trust the answer He gives.

Have you prayed about your resources lately?
Find out how God wants you to use your time and
your money. No matter what it costs,
forsake all that is not of God.

KAY ARTHUR

The most important business I'm engaged in ought
to be the Lord's business. If it ain't, I need to get off
and classify myself and see whose side I'm on.

JERRY CLOWER

The best and most beautiful things
in this world cannot be seen or even heard.
They must be felt with the heart.

HELEN KELLER

Often our lives are strangled by things
that don't ultimately matter.

GRADY NUTT

God is everything. My focus must be on him,
seeking to know him more completely and
allowing him full possession of my life.

MARY MORRISON SUGGS

MORE FROM GOD'S WORD

Let us fix our eyes on Jesus, the author and
perfecter of our faith, who for the joy set before him
endured the cross, scorning its shame,
and sat down at the right hand of the throne of God.

HEBREWS 12:2 NIV

TODAY, I WILL THINK ABOUT . . .

The need to allow God's priorities
to become my priorities.

A PRAYER TO START MY DAY

Lord, let Your priorities be my priorities.
Let Your will be my will. Let Your Word be
my guide, and let me grow in faith and
in wisdom this day and every day. —Amen

WHOM WILL YOU ENCOURAGE TODAY?

WATCH THE WAY YOU TALK.
LET NOTHING FOUL OR DIRTY COME OUT
OF YOUR MOUTH. SAY ONLY WHAT HELPS,
EACH WORD A GIFT.

EPHESIANS 4:29 MSG

Life is a team sport, and all of us need occasional pats on the back from our teammates. As Christians, we are called upon to spread the Good News of Christ, and we are also called to spread a message of encouragement and hope to the world.

In the book of Ephesians, Paul writes, "Do not let any unwholesome talk come out of your mouths, but only what is helpful for building others up according to their needs, that it may benefit those who listen" (4:29 NIV). Paul reminds us that when we choose our words carefully, we can have a powerful impact on those around us.

Whether you realize it or not, many people with whom you come in contact every day are in desperate need of a smile or an encouraging word. The world can be a difficult place, and countless friends and family members may be troubled by the challenges of everyday life. Since we don't always know who needs our help, the best strategy is to encourage all the people who cross our paths. So today, be a world-class source of encouragement to everyone you meet. Never has the need been greater.

Do you wonder where you can go for
encouragement and motivation? Run to Jesus.

MAX LUCADO

Encouragement is to a friendship
what confetti is to a party.

NICOLE JOHNSON

The truest help we can render an afflicted man is
not to take his burden from him,
but to call out his best energy, that he may be able
to bear the burden himself.

PHILLIPS BROOKS

A hug is the ideal gift . . . one size fits all.

ANONYMOUS

The secret of success is to find a need and fill it,
to find a hurt and heal it, to find somebody
with a problem and offer to help solve it.

ROBERT SCHULLER

MORE FROM GOD'S WORD

Let the word of Christ dwell in you richly in all wisdom;
teaching and admonishing one another in psalms
and hymns and spiritual songs,
singing with grace in your hearts to the Lord.

COLOSSIANS 3:16 KJV

TODAY, I WILL THINK ABOUT . . .

The impact that my encouragement
has upon others.

A PRAYER TO START MY DAY

Dear Heavenly Father, because I am Your child,
I am blessed. You have loved me eternally,
cared for me faithfully, and saved me through
the gift of Your Son Jesus. Just as You have lifted
me up, Lord, let me lift up others in a spirit of
encouragement and optimism and hope.
And, if I can help a fellow traveler, even in a small
way, dear Lord, may the glory be Yours. —Amen

A HUMBLE HEART

DO NOTHING OUT OF RIVALRY OR CONCEIT,
BUT IN HUMILITY CONSIDER OTHERS
AS MORE IMPORTANT THAN YOURSELVES.

PHILIPPIANS 2:3 HCSB

As fallible human beings, we have so much to be humble about. Why, then, is humility such a difficult trait for us to master? Precisely because we are fallible human beings. Yet if we are to grow and mature as Christians, we must strive to give credit where credit is due, starting, of course, with God and His only begotten Son.

As Christians, we have been refashioned and saved by Jesus Christ, and that salvation came not because of our own good works but because of God's grace. Thus, we are not "self-made"; we are "God-made," and we are "Christ-saved." How, then, can we be boastful? The answer, of course, is that, if we are honest with ourselves and with our God, we simply can't be boastful . . . we must, instead, be eternally grateful and exceedingly humble. Humility, however, is not easy for most of us. All too often, we are tempted to stick out our chests and say, "Look at me; look what I did!" But, in the quiet moments when we search the depths of our own hearts, we know better. Whatever "it" is, God did that. And He deserves the credit.

Humility is a grace in the soul.
It is indescribable wealth,
a name and a gift from God.

JOHN CLIMACUS

Let us humble our hearts before
the Lord and seek his help and approval
above all other things.

JIM CYMBALA

Humility trains us to recognize God's supremacy,
to view ourselves as his creatures,
to see him as the Potter, ourselves as clay.

JAN WINEBRENNER

We see how Jesus clearly chooses the way of
humility. He does not appear with great fanfare as
a powerful savior, announcing a new order.
On the contrary, he comes quietly,
with the many sinners who are receiving
a baptism of repentance.

HENRI NOUWEN

MORE FROM GOD'S WORD

*If My people who are called by My name will
humble themselves, and pray and seek My face,
and turn from their wicked ways, then I will hear from
heaven, and will forgive their sin and heal their land.*

2 CHRONICLES 7:14 NKJV

TODAY, I WILL THINK ABOUT . . .

The need to humbly thank God
for His countless blessings.

A PRAYER TO START MY DAY

Heavenly Father, it is the nature of mankind to
be prideful, and I am no exception. When I am
boastful, Lord, keep me mindful that all my gifts
come from You. When I feel prideful, remind me
that You sent Your Son to be a humble carpenter
and that Jesus was ridiculed and crucified on a cross.
Let me grow beyond my need for earthly praise,
God, and let me look only to You for approval.
You are the Giver of all things good; let me give
all the glory to You. —Amen

WHEN THE DAY IS DIFFICULT

COME TO ME, ALL YOU WHO LABOR AND
ARE HEAVY LADEN, AND I WILL GIVE YOU REST.
TAKE MY YOKE UPON YOU AND LEARN FROM
ME, FOR I AM GENTLE AND LOWLY IN HEART,
AND YOU WILL FIND REST FOR YOUR SOULS.
FOR MY YOKE IS EASY AND
MY BURDEN IS LIGHT.

MATTHEW 11:28-30 NKJV

Allll of us face those occasional days when the traffic jams and the dog gobbles the homework. But, when we find ourselves overtaken by the minor frustrations of life, we must catch ourselves, take a deep breath, and lift our thoughts upward. Although we are here on earth struggling to rise above the distractions of the day, we need never struggle alone. God is here—eternally and faithfully, with infinite patience and love—and, if we reach out to Him, He will restore perspective and peace to our souls.

Sometimes even the most devout Christians can become discouraged, and you are no exception. After all, you live in a world where expectations can be high and demands can be even higher.

If, today, you find yourself enduring difficult circumstances, remember that God remains in His heaven. If you become discouraged with the direction of your day or your life, lift your thoughts and prayers to Him. He is a God of possibility, not negativity. He will guide you through your difficulties and beyond them. Then, you can thank the Giver of all things good for blessings that are simply too numerous to count.

Anyone can carry his burden, however hard,
until nightfall. Anyone can do his work, however
hard, for one day. Anyone can live sweetly,
patiently, lovingly, purely, till the sun goes down.
And this is all that life really means.

ROBERT LOUIS STEVENSON

God does not dispense strength and encouragement
like a druggist fills your prescription.
The Lord doesn't promise to give us something to
take so we can handle our weary moments.
He promises us Himself. That is all.
And that is enough.

CHARLES SWINDOLL

We should not be upset when unexpected and
upsetting things happen. God, in his wisdom,
means to make something of us which we have not
yet attained, and He is dealing with us accordingly.

J. I. PACKER

It is impossible for that man to despair who
remembers that his helper is omnipotent.

JEREMY TAYLOR

MORE FROM GOD'S WORD

Consider it pure joy, my brothers, whenever you
face trials of many kinds, because you know that
the testing of your faith develops perseverance.
Perseverance must finish its work so that you may be
mature and complete, not lacking anything.

JAMES 1:2-4 NIV

TODAY, I WILL THINK ABOUT . . .

The strength that can be mine when I allow
Christ to dwell in the center of my heart.

A PRAYER TO START MY DAY

Dear Heavenly Father, when I am troubled,
You heal me. When I am afraid, You protect me.
When I am discouraged, You lift me up. You are my
unending source of strength, Lord; let me turn to
You when I am weak. In the difficult days of my life,
let me trust Your plan and Your will. And whatever
my circumstances, Lord, let me always give
the thanks and the glory to You. —Amen

ENCOUNTERING GOD IN THE HERE AND NOW

DRAW NEAR TO GOD,
AND HE WILL DRAW NEAR TO YOU.

JAMES 4:8 HCSB

As you think about the day ahead, here's an important question to ask yourself: do you expect God to walk with you every step of the way? The answer to that question, of course, has nothing to do with God and everything to do with you. God will most certainly be there for you . . . will you be there with Him?

When you begin the day with prayer and praise, God often seems very near indeed. But, if you ignore God's presence or—worse yet—rebel against it altogether, the world in which you live becomes a spiritual wasteland.

Are you tired, discouraged or fearful? Be comforted because God is with you. Are you confused? Listen to the quiet voice of your Heavenly Father. Are you bitter? Talk with God and seek His guidance. Are you celebrating a great victory? Thank God and praise Him. He is the Giver of all things good.

In whatever condition you find yourself, whether you are happy or sad, victorious or vanquished, troubled or triumphant, celebrate God's presence. And be comforted. God is not just near. He is here.

I have a capacity in my soul for taking in God
entirely. I am as sure as I live that nothing is so near
to me as God. God is nearer to me than I am
to myself; my existence depends on
the nearness and the presence of God.

MEISTER ECKHART

Whatever we have done in the past, be it good or
evil, great or small, is irrelevant to our stance
before God today. It is only now that
we are in the presence of God.

BRENNAN MANNING

There is a God-shaped vacuum in the heart of
every person, and it can never be filled by
any created thing. It can only be filled by God,
made known through Jesus Christ.

BLAISE PASCAL

Pour out your heart to God and tell Him
how you feel. Be real, be honest, and when
you get it all out, you'll start to feel the gradual
covering of God's comforting presence.

BILL HYBELS

MORE FROM GOD'S WORD

*Be strong and courageous. Do not be terrified;
do not be discouraged, for the LORD your God
will be with you wherever you go.*

JOSHUA 1:9 NIV

TODAY, I WILL THINK ABOUT . . .

The need to seek God's presence *and* the wisdom
of allowing God to influence
my decisions throughout the day.

A PRAYER TO START MY DAY

Heavenly Father, help me to feel Your presence
in every situation and every circumstance.
You are with me, Lord, in times of celebration and
in times of sorrow. You are with me when
I am strong and when I am weak. You never leave
my side even when it seems to me that You are far
away. Today and every day, God, let me feel
You and acknowledge Your presence so that others,
too, might know You through me. —Amen

WISDOM FOR TODAY

WISDOM IS A TREE OF LIFE
TO THOSE WHO EMBRACE HER;
HAPPY ARE THOSE WHO HOLD HER TIGHTLY.

PROVERBS 3:18 NLT

Where will you find wisdom today? Will you seek it from God or from the world? As a thoughtful man living in a society that is filled with temptations and distractions, you know that the world's brand of "wisdom" is everywhere . . . and it is dangerous. You live in a world where it's all too easy to stray far from the ultimate source of wisdom: God's Holy Word.

When you commit yourself to daily study of God's Word—and when you live according to His commandments—you will become wise . . . in time. But don't expect to open your Bible today and be wise tomorrow. Wisdom is not like a mushroom; it does not spring up overnight. It is, instead, like a majestic oak tree that starts as a tiny acorn, grows into a sapling, and eventually reaches up to the sky, tall and strong.

Today and every day, as a way of understanding God's plan for your life, you should study His Word and live by it. When you do, you will accumulate a storehouse of wisdom that will enrich your own life and the lives of your family members, your friends, and the world.

If you lack knowledge, go to school.
If you lack wisdom, get on your knees.

VANCE HAVNER

Wisdom is the foundation, and justice is the work
without which a foundation cannot stand.

ST. AMBROSE

The person who is wise spiritually, who is
a true Christian, builds his life and performs
his duties carefully, realizing the great substance
and importance involved.

JOHN MACARTHUR

Wisdom is the God-given ability to see life
with rare objectivity and to handle life
with rare stability.

CHARLES SWINDOLL

Wisdom is the right use of knowledge.
To know is not to be wise. Many men know
a great deal, and are all the greater fools for it.
But to know how to use knowledge
is to have wisdom.

C. H. SPURGEON

MORE FROM GOD'S WORD

The fear of the LORD is the beginning of wisdom;
a good understanding have all those who do
His commandments. His praise endures forever.

PSALM 111:10 NKJV

Happy is the person who finds wisdom
and gains understanding.

PROVERBS 3:13 NLT

TODAY, I WILL THINK ABOUT . . .

The difference between the world's "wisdom"
and God's true wisdom.

A PRAYER TO START MY DAY

Dear Lord, when I depend upon the world's wisdom,
I make many mistakes. But when I trust in
Your wisdom, I build my life on a firm foundation.
Today and every day I will trust Your Word and
follow it, knowing that the ultimate wisdom is
Your wisdom and the ultimate truth
is Your truth. —Amen

THE POWER OF PERSEVERANCE

LET US THROW OFF EVERYTHING THAT
HINDERS AND THE SIN THAT SO EASILY
ENTANGLES, AND LET US RUN WITH
PERSEVERANCE THE RACE
MARKED OUT FOR US.

HEBREWS 12:1 NIV

A well-lived life is like a marathon, not a sprint—it calls for preparation, determination, and lots of perseverance. As an example of perfect perseverance, we Christians need look no further than our Savior, Jesus Christ.

Jesus finished what He began. Despite His suffering, despite the shame of the cross, Jesus was steadfast in His faithfulness to God. We, too, must remain faithful, especially during times of hardship. Sometimes, God may answer our prayers with silence, and when He does, we must patiently persevere.

Are you facing a difficult time in your life? If so, remember the words of Winston Churchill: "Never give in!" And remember this: whatever your problem, God can handle it. Your job is to keep persevering until He does.

Battles are won in the trenches,
in the grit and grime of courageous determination;
they are won day by day in the arena of life.

CHARLES SWINDOLL

Only the man who follows the command of
Jesus single-mindedly and unresistingly lets his yoke
rest upon him, finds his burden easy,
and under its gentle pressure receives
the power to persevere in the right way.

DIETRICH BONHOEFFER

All rising to a great place is by a winding stair.

FRANCIS BACON

Let us not cease to do the utmost, that we may
incessantly go forward in the way of the Lord;
and let us not despair of the smallness
of our accomplishments.

JOHN CALVIN

MORE FROM GOD'S WORD

*Let us not become weary in doing good,
for at the proper time we will reap a harvest
if we do not give up.*

GALATIANS 6:9 NIV

TODAY, I WILL THINK ABOUT . . .

The need for perseverance and courage.

A PRAYER TO START MY DAY

Lord, when life is difficult, I am tempted to abandon
hope in the future. But You are my God,
and I can draw strength from You. Let me
trust You, Father, in good times and in bad times.
Let me persevere—even if my soul is troubled—
and let me follow Your Son Jesus Christ
this day and forever. —Amen

A DAY FILLED WITH LAUGHER

THERE IS A TIME FOR EVERYTHING, AND EVERYTHING ON EARTH HAS ITS SPECIAL SEASON . . . . THERE IS A TIME TO CRY AND A TIME TO LAUGH. THERE IS A TIME TO BE SAD AND A TIME TO DANCE.

ECCLESIASTES 3:1,4 NCV

Laughter is medicine for the soul, but sometimes, amid the stresses of the day, we forget to take our medicine. Instead of viewing our world with a mixture of optimism and humor, we allow worries and distractions to rob us of the joy that God intends for our lives.

So the next time you find yourself dwelling upon the negatives of life, refocus your attention to things positive. The next time you find yourself falling prey to the blight of pessimism, stop yourself and turn your thoughts around. And, if you see your glass as "half-empty," rest assured that your spiritual vision is impaired. With God, your glass is never half-empty. With God as your protector and Christ as your Savior, your glass is filled to the brim and overflowing . . . forever.

Today, as you go about your daily activities, approach life with a smile on your lips and hope in your heart. And laugh every chance you get. After all, God created laughter for a reason . . . and Father indeed knows best. So laugh!

A keen sense of humor helps us to overlook
the unbecoming, understand the unconventional,
tolerate the unpleasant, overcome the unexpected,
and outlast the unbearable.

BILLY GRAHAM

I want to encourage you in these days with
your family to lighten up and enjoy.
Laugh a little bit; it might just set you free.

DENNIS SWANBERG

Let laughter reign when it comes.
It is oil for the engines that rise to
challenges and work miracles.

DONALD E. DEMARAY

Mirth is God's medicine.
Everybody ought to bathe in it.

HENRY WARD BEECHER

I think everybody ought to be a laughing Christian.
I'm convinced that there's just one place where
there's not any laughter, and that's hell.

JERRY CLOWER

MORE FROM GOD'S WORD

A cheerful heart is good medicine.

PROVERBS 17:22 NIV

*. . . as the occasion when Jews got relief from their
enemies, the month in which their sorrow turned to joy,
mourning somersaulted into a holiday for parties
and fun and laughter, the sending and receiving of
presents and of giving gifts to the poor.*

ESTHER 9:22 MSG

TODAY, I WILL THINK ABOUT . . .

Ways that I can use humor to improve
my own life and the lives of the people around me.

A PRAYER TO START MY DAY

Dear Lord, laughter is Your gift.
Today and every day, put a smile on my face,
and let me share that smile with all who cross
my path . . . and let me laugh. —Amen

HOW WILL YOU LEAD?

GOOD LEADERSHIP IS A CHANNEL OF WATER
CONTROLLED BY GOD;
HE DIRECTS IT TO WHATEVER ENDS
HE CHOOSES.

PROVERBS 21:1 MSG

Our world needs Christian leaders who willingly honor God with their words and their deeds, but not necessarily in that order.

If you seek to be a godly leader, then you must begin by being a worthy example to your family, to your friends, to your church, and to your community. After all, your words of instruction will never ring true unless you yourself are willing to follow them.

Christ-centered leadership is an exercise in service: service to God in heaven and service to His children here on earth. Christ willingly became a servant to His followers, and you must seek to do the same for yours.

Are you the kind of servant-leader whom you would want to follow? If so, congratulations: you are honoring your Savior by imitating Him. And that, of course, is the sincerest form of flattery.

Only He can guide you to invest your life in worthwhile ways. This guidance will come as you "walk" with Him and listen to Him.

HENRY BLACKABY AND CLAUDE KING

Men give advice; God gives guidance.

LEONARD RAVENHILL

Integrity and maturity are two character traits vital to the heart of a leader.

CHARLES STANLEY

You can never separate a leader's actions from his character.

JOHN MAXWELL

As we trust God to give us wisdom for today's decisions, He will lead us a step at a time into what He wants us to be doing in the future.

THEODORE EPP

MORE FROM GOD'S WORD

*In all your ways acknowledge Him, and He shall direct
your paths.*

PROVERBS 3:6 NKJV

*The true children of God are those who let God's Spirit
lead them.*

ROMANS 8:14 NCV

TODAY, I WILL THINK ABOUT . . .

Ways that I can follow Christ—
and I will think about ways that I can encourage
others to do the same.

A PRAYER TO START MY DAY

Dear Lord, You always stand ready to guide me.
Let me accept Your guidance, today and every day
of my life. Lead me, Father, and let me trust You
completely, so that my life can be a tribute to
Your grace, to Your mercy, to Your love,
and to Your Son. —Amen

THE OPPORTUNITY TO FORGIVE

BE KIND TO EACH OTHER, TENDERHEARTED,
FORGIVING ONE ANOTHER,
JUST AS GOD THROUGH CHRIST
HAS FORGIVEN YOU.

EPHESIANS 4:32 NLT

As you make plans for the day ahead, here's a question: whom do you need to forgive today?

If you're like most folks, you probably find it difficult to forgive the people who have harmed you. No matter. As a Christian, you are *commanded* to forgive others, just as you, too, have been forgiven. So even when forgiveness is difficult, you must ask God to help you move beyond the spiritual stumbling blocks of bitterness, anger, hatred, and regret.

When you forgive those who have hurt you, then you most certainly honor God by obeying His commandments. But when you harbor bitterness against others, your disobedience brings suffering— needless suffering—upon you and your loved ones.

Today provides yet another opportunity to cleanse your heart by forgiving the people who have hurt you. So, if you hold bitterness against even a single person, forgive. If there exists even one person, alive or dead, whom you have not forgiven, follow God's commandment and His will for your life: forgive. If you are embittered against yourself for some past mistake or shortcoming, forgive. Then, to the best of your abilities, forget. And move on. Bitterness and regret are not part of God's plan for your life. Forgiveness is.

The sequence of forgiveness and then repentance, rather than repentance and then forgiveness, is crucial for understanding the gospel of grace.

BRENNAN MANNING

Jesus had a forgiving and understanding heart. If he lives within us, mercy will temper our relationships with our fellow men.

BILLY GRAHAM

I firmly believe a great many prayers are not answered because we are not willing to forgive someone.

D. L. MOODY

Forgiving is a gift God has given us for healing ourselves before we are ready to help anyone else.

DR. LEWIS SMEDES

Having forgiven, I am liberated.

FATHER LAWRENCE JENCO

MORE FROM GOD'S WORD

Then Peter came to him and asked,
"Lord, how often should I forgive someone who
sins against me? Seven times?"
"No!" Jesus replied, "seventy times seven!"

MATTHEW 18:21-22 NLT

TODAY, I WILL THINK ABOUT . . .

The people whom I still need to forgive.

A PRAYER TO START MY DAY

Dear Lord, when I am bitter, You can change
my unforgiving heart. And, when I am slow
to forgive, Your Word reminds me that forgiveness
is Your commandment. Let me be Your obedient
servant, Lord, and let me forgive others just
as You have forgiven me. —Amen

AND THE GREATEST OF THESE . . .

NOW THESE THREE REMAIN:
FAITH, HOPE, AND LOVE.
BUT THE GREATEST OF THESE IS LOVE.

1 CORINTHIANS 13:13 HCSB

Christ's words left no room for interpretation: "'Love the Lord your God with all your heart and with all your soul and with all your mind.' This is the first and greatest commandment. And the second is like it: 'Love your neighbor as yourself.' All the Law and the Prophets hang on these two commandments" (Matthew 22:37-40 NIV). But sometimes, despite our best intentions, we fall short. When we become embittered with ourselves, with our neighbors, or most especially with God, we disobey the One who gave His life for us.

If we are to please God, we must cleanse ourselves of the negative feelings that separate us from others and from Him. In 1 Corinthians 13, we are told that love is the foundation upon which all our relationships are to be built: our relationships with others and our relationship with our Maker. May we fill our hearts with love; may we never yield to bitterness. And may we praise the Son of God who, in His infinite wisdom, made love His greatest commandment.

Love is responsibility.

MARTIN BUBER

Faith, like light, should always be simple and
unbending; love, like warmth, should beam
forth on every side and bend to every necessity
of our brethren.

MARTIN LUTHER

A little rain can strengthen a flower stem.
A little love can change a life.

MAX LUCADO

They'll know we are Christians by our love.

PETER SCHOLTES

Service is love in overalls!

ANONYMOUS

MORE FROM GOD'S WORD

*A new commandment I give to you,
that you love one another; as I have loved you,
that you also love one another.*

JOHN 13:34 NKJV

*Greater love has no one than this,
than to lay down one's life for his friends.*

JOHN 15:13 NKJV

TODAY, I WILL THINK ABOUT . . .

Ways that I can use both words and deeds to
demonstrate the love that I feel in my heart for
others.

A PRAYER TO START MY DAY

Dear Lord, You have given me the gift of love;
let me share that gift with others. And, keep me
mindful that the essence of love is not to receive it,
but to give it, today and forever. —Amen

GENUINE PEACE

AND THE PEACE OF GOD,
WHICH TRANSCENDS ALL UNDERSTANDING,
WILL GUARD YOUR HEARTS AND
YOUR MINDS IN CHRIST JESUS.

PHILIPPIANS 4:7 NIV

What are you expecting from the day ahead? Do you expect to enjoy peace and abundance, or do you fear that your day will be filled with stress and strain?

If you hope to experience peace—a lasting sense of peace that helps you rise above the inevitable struggles of daily living—then you must make God a partner in every aspect of your life.

When you accept the genuine peace that flows from God and from His only begotten Son, then you can share that peace with fellow Christians, family members, friends, and associates. If, on the other hand, you choose to ignore the gift of peace—for whatever reason—you simply cannot share what you do not possess.

Today, as a gift to yourself, to your family, and to your friends, claim the inner peace that is your spiritual birthright: the peace of Jesus Christ. It is offered freely; it has been paid for in full; it is yours for the asking. So ask. And then share.

If our minds are stayed upon God,
His peace will rule the affairs entertained
by our minds. If, on the other hand, we allow
our minds to dwell on the cares of this world,
God's peace will be far from our thoughts.

WOODROLL KROLL

We're prone to want God to change
our circumstances, but He wants to change
our character. We think that peace comes from
the outside in, but it comes from the inside out.

WARREN WIERSBE

Where the Spirit of the Lord is, there is peace;
where the Spirit of the Lord is, there is love.

STEPHEN R. ADAMS

Put God underneath all your life,
and your life must rest upon the everlasting arms.

PHILLIPS BROOKS

MORE FROM GOD'S WORD

Let the peace of Christ rule in your hearts,
since as members of one body you were called to peace.

COLOSSIANS 3:15 NIV

You, Lord, give true peace to those who depend on you,
because they trust you.

ISAIAH 26:3 NCV

TODAY, I WILL THINK ABOUT . . .

The genuine peace that can—and should—be mine
when I welcome Christ into my heart.

A PRAYER TO START MY DAY

Dear Lord, I will open my heart to You.
And I thank You, God, for Your love,
for Your peace, and for Your Son. —Amen

THE TEMPTATIONS OF EVERYDAY LIFE

No temptation has seized you
except what is common to man.
And God is faithful; he will not let you
be tempted beyond what you can bear.
But when you are tempted,
he will also provide a way out so that
you can stand up under it.

1 Corinthians 10:13 NIV

It's inevitable: today you will be tempted by somebody or something—in fact, you will probably be tempted many times. Why? Because you live in a world that is filled to the brim with temptations! Some of these temptations are small; eating a second scoop of ice cream, for example, is enticing but not very dangerous. Other temptations, however, are not nearly so harmless.

The devil is working 24/7, and he's causing pain and heartache in more ways than ever before. We, as believers, must remain watchful and strong. And the good news is this: When it comes to fighting Satan, we are never alone. God is always with us, and He gives us the power to resist temptation whenever we ask Him to give us strength.

In a letter to believers, Peter offered a stern warning: "Your adversary, the devil, prowls around like a roaring lion, seeking someone to devour" (I Peter 5:8 NASB). As Christians, we must take that warning seriously, and we must behave accordingly.

I believe with all my heart and soul that at
every important crossroads in my life I was faced
with a choice: between right and wrong,
between serving God and pleasing myself.
I didn't always make the right choice. In fact,
I stumbled down the wrong path more times than
I marched down the right one. But God heard
the earnest prayers of those who loved me and
by His grace brought me to my knees.

AL GREEN

Man without God is always torn between
two urges. His nature prompts him to do wrong,
and his conscience urges him to do right.
Christ can rid you of that inner conflict.

BILLY GRAHAM

The higher the hill, the stronger the wind:
so the loftier the life,
the stronger the enemy's temptations.

JOHN WYCLIFFE

It is easier to stay out of temptation
than to get out of it.

RICK WARREN

MORE FROM GOD'S WORD

*Watch and pray so that you will not fall into temptation.
The spirit is willing but the body is weak.*

MATTHEW 26:41 NIV

TODAY, I WILL THINK ABOUT . . .

My need to avoid people and places that might
cause me to stray from God's plan for my life.

A PRAYER TO START MY DAY

Dear Lord, this world is filled with temptations,
distractions, and frustrations. When I turn
my thoughts away from You and Your Word, Lord,
I suffer bitter consequences. But, when I trust in
Your commandments, I am safe. Direct my path far
from the temptations and distractions of the world.
Let me discover Your will and follow it, dear Lord,
this day and always. —Amen

MAKING THE MOST OF YOUR TALENTS TODAY

NEGLECT NOT THE GIFT THAT IS IN THEE . . . .

1 TIMOTHY 4:14 KJV

The old saying is both familiar and true: "What we are is God's gift to us; what we become is our gift to God." Each of us possesses special talents, gifted by God, that can be nurtured carefully or ignored totally. Our challenge, of course, is to use our abilities to the greatest extent possible and to use them in ways that honor our Savior.

As you plan for the day ahead, are you planning to use your talents to make God's world a better place? If so, congratulations. But if you have gifts that you have not fully explored and developed, perhaps you need to have a chat with the One who gave you those gifts in the first place.

Your talents are priceless treasures offered from your Heavenly Father. Use them. After all, an obvious way to say "thank you" to the Giver is to use the gifts He has given.

You are a unique blend of talents, skills, and gifts,
which makes you an indispensable member
of the body of Christ.

CHARLES STANLEY

Natural abilities are like natural plants;
they need pruning by study.

FRANCIS BACON

Discipline is the refining fire
by which talent becomes ability.

ROY L. SMITH

You are the only person on earth
who can use your ability.

ZIG ZIGLAR

One thing taught large in the Holy Scriptures is
that while God gives His gifts freely, He will require
a strict accounting of them at the end of the road.
Each man is personally responsible for his store,
be it large or small, and will be required to explain
his use of it before the judgment seat of Christ.

A. W. TOZER

MORE FROM GOD'S WORD

We have different gifts, according to the grace given us. If a man's gift is prophesying, let him use it in proportion to his faith. If it is serving, let him serve; if it is teaching, let him teach; if it is encouraging, let him encourage; if it is contributing to the needs of others, let him give generously; if it is leadership, let him govern diligently; if it is showing mercy, let him do it cheerfully.

ROMANS 12:6-8 NIV

TODAY, I WILL THINK ABOUT . . .

Ways that I can convert my talents into results.

A PRAYER TO START MY DAY

Father, You have given me abilities to be used for the glory of Your kingdom. Give me the courage and the perseverance to use those talents. Keep me mindful that all my gifts come from You, Lord. Let me be Your faithful, humble servant, and let me give You all the glory and all the praise. —Amen

HAPPINESS NOW

PRAISE THE LORD!
HAPPY ARE THOSE WHO RESPECT THE LORD,
WHO WANT WHAT HE COMMANDS.

PSALM 112:1 NCV

D o you seek happiness, abundance, and contentment? And do you seek these things now, not later? If so, here's what you should do: Love God and His Son; depend upon God for strength; try, to the best of your abilities, to follow God's will; and strive to obey His Holy Word. When you do these things, you'll discover that happiness goes hand-in-hand with righteousness.

The happiest people are not those who rebel against God; the happiest people are those who love God and obey His commandments. If you sincerely want to be happy, you should behave accordingly.

What should you expect from the upcoming day? A world full of possibilities (of course it's up to you to seize them), and God's promise of abundance (of course it's up to you to accept it). So, as you prepare for the next step in your life's journey, remember this: obedience to God doesn't ensure instant happiness, but disobedience to God always makes genuine happiness impossible.

The secret of a happy life is to delight in duty.
When duty becomes delight,
then burdens become blessings.

WARREN WIERSBE

To be in a state of true grace is to be miserable
no more; it is to be happy forever.
A soul in this state is a soul near and dear to God.
It is a soul housed in God.

THOMAS BROOKS

The secret of a happy life is to do your duty and
trust in God.

SAM JONES

There is no correlation between
wealth and happiness.

LARRY BURKETT

God made round faces; man makes 'em long.

ANONYMOUS

MORE FROM GOD'S WORD

So I recommend having fun, because there is nothing better for people to do in this world than to eat, drink, and enjoy life. That way they will experience some happiness along with all the hard work God gives them.

ECCLESIASTES 8:15 NLT

Those who are pure in their thinking are happy, because they will be with God.

MATTHEW 5:8 NCV

TODAY, I WILL THINK ABOUT . . .

The happiness and abundance that can be mine when I obey God's commandments.

A PRAYER TO START MY DAY

Dear Lord, I am thankful for all the blessings You have given me. Let me be a happy Christian, Father, as I share Your joy with friends, with family, and with the world. —Amen

A DAY FILLED WITH PRAYER

REJOICE ALWAYS, PRAY WITHOUT CEASING,
IN EVERYTHING GIVE THANKS;
FOR THIS IS THE WILL OF GOD
IN CHRIST JESUS FOR YOU.

1 THESSALONIANS 5:16-18 NKJV

On his second missionary journey, Paul started a small church in Thessalonica. A short time later, he penned a letter that was intended to encourage the new believers at that church. Today, almost 2,000 years later, 1 Thessalonians remains a powerful, practical guide for Christian living.

In his letter, Paul advises members of the new church to "pray without ceasing." His advice applies to Christians of every generation. When we weave the habit of prayer into the very fabric of our days, we invite God to become a partner in every aspect of our lives. When we consult God on an hourly basis, we avail ourselves of His wisdom, His strength, and His love. When we pray without ceasing, we enrich our own lives and the lives of those around us.

Today, instead of turning things over in your mind, turn them over to God in prayer. Instead of worrying about your next decision, ask God to lead the way. Don't limit your prayers to meals or bedtime. Pray constantly about things great and small. God is listening, and He wants to hear from you. Now.

O, let the place of secret prayer become to me
the most beloved spot on earth.

ANDREW MURRAY

The most effective thing we can do for our children
and families is to pray for them.

ANTHONY EVANS

The more praying there is in the world,
the better the world will be,
the mightier the forces against evil everywhere.

E. M. BOUNDS

Prayer is fundamentally and essentially
self-surrender, not a method of obtaining
from God your wishes.

E. STANLEY JONES

Prayer is life passionately wanting, wishing, desiring
God's triumph. Prayer is life striving and toiling
everywhere and always for that ultimate victory.

G. CAMPBELL MORGAN

MORE FROM GOD'S WORD

*If you don't know what you're doing, pray to
the Father. He loves to help. You'll get his help,
and won't be condescended to when you ask for it.
Ask boldly, believingly, without a second thought.
People who "worry their prayers" are like wind-whipped
waves. Don't think you're going to get anything
from the Master that way, adrift at sea,
keeping all your options open.*

JAMES 1:5-8 MSG

TODAY, I WILL THINK ABOUT . . .

The role that prayer plays in my life.

A PRAYER TO START MY DAY

Dear Lord, make me a person whose constant
prayers are pleasing to You. Let me come to You
often with concerns both great and small. And,
when You answer my prayers, Father, let me trust
Your answers, today and forever. —Amen

THE POWER OF PURPOSE

YOU WILL SHOW ME THE PATH OF LIFE;
IN YOUR PRESENCE IS FULLNESS OF JOY;
AT YOUR RIGHT HAND ARE
PLEASURES FOREVERMORE.

PSALM 16:11 NKJV

God has plans for your life, but He won't force those plans upon you. To the contrary, He has given you free will, the ability to make decisions on your own. With that freedom to choose comes the responsibility of living with the consequences of the choices you make.

If you seek to live in accordance with God's will for your life—and you should—then you will contemplate His Word, and you will be watchful for His signs. You will associate with fellow Christians who will encourage your spiritual growth, and you will listen to that inner voice that speaks to you in the quiet moments of your daily devotionals.

God intends to use you in wonderful, unexpected ways if you let Him, but be forewarned: the decision to seek God's plan and fulfill His purpose is yours and yours alone. The consequences of that decision have implications that are both profound and eternal, so choose carefully. And, as you go about your daily activities, keep your eyes and ears open . . . as well as your heart.

Without God, life has no purpose,
and without purpose, life has no meaning.

RICK WARREN

Their distress is due entirely to their deliberate
determination to use themselves for
a purpose other than God's.

OSWALD CHAMBERS

Have I today done anything to fulfill the purpose
for which Thou didst cause me to be born?

JOHN BAILLIE

When God speaks to you through the Bible,
prayer, circumstances, the church, or in some other
way, he has a purpose in mind for your life.

HENRY BLACKABY AND CLAUDE KING

The place where God calls you is the place
where your deep gladness and
the world's deep hunger meet.

FREDERICK BUECHNER

MORE FROM GOD'S WORD

To everything there is a season,
a time for every purpose under heaven.

ECCLESIASTES 3:1 NKJV

God chose you to be his people, so I urge you now
to live the life to which God called you.

EPHESIANS 4:1 NCV

TODAY, I WILL THINK ABOUT . . .

The importance of living purposefully,
not accidentally.

A PRAYER TO START MY DAY

Lord, You've got something You want me
to do—help me to figure out exactly what it is.
Give me Your blessings and lead me along
a path that is pleasing to You . . .
today, tomorrow, and forever. —Amen

WHAT KIND OF EXAMPLE WILL YOU BE TODAY?

YOU ARE THE LIGHT THAT GIVES LIGHT TO THE WORLD. IN THE SAME WAY, YOU SHOULD BE A LIGHT FOR OTHER PEOPLE. LIVE SO THAT THEY WILL SEE THE GOOD THINGS YOU DO AND WILL PRAISE YOUR FATHER IN HEAVEN.

MATTHEW 5:14,16 NCV

What kind of example will you be today? The answer to this question will determine, in large part, whether or not you will be a positive influence on your own little corner of the world.

Are you the kind of man whose life serves as a powerful example of righteousness? Are you a person whose behavior serves as a positive role model for others? Are you the kind of Christian whose actions, day in and day out, are based upon integrity, fidelity, and a love for the Lord? If so, you are not only blessed by God, but you are also a powerful force for good in a world that desperately needs positive influences such as yours.

Phillips Brooks advised, "Be such a man, and live such a life, that if every person were such as you, and every life a life like yours, this earth would be God's Paradise." And that's sound advice because your family and friends are watching . . . and so, for that matter, is God.

Be careful how you live.
You may be the only Bible some person ever reads.

WILLIAM J. TOMS

Live to explain thy doctrine by thy life.

MATTHEW PRIOR

You can preach a better sermon with your life
than with your lips.

OLIVER GOLDSMITH

A person who lives right and is right has more
power in his silence than another has by words.

PHILLIPS BROOKS

It's good to be saved and know it!
It's also good to be saved and show it!

ANONYMOUS

MORE FROM GOD'S WORD

*In everything set them an example by doing
what is good.*

TITUS 2:7 NIV

*You should be an example to the believers in speech,
in conduct, in love, in faith, in purity.*

1 TIMOTHY 4:12 HCSB

TODAY, I WILL THINK ABOUT . . .

Ways that my own behavior impacts
my family and friends.

A PRAYER TO START MY DAY

Lord, make me a worthy example to my family and
friends. And, let my words and my actions show
people how my life has been changed by You.
I will praise You, Father, by following
in the footsteps of Your Son.
Let others see Him through me. —Amen

THE MAGIC OF THE MORNING

EVERY MORNING HE WAKES ME.

HE TEACHES ME TO LISTEN LIKE A STUDENT.

THE LORD GOD HELPS ME LEARN . . . .

ISAIAH 50:4-5 NCV

Each new day is a gift from God, and if we are wise, we will spend a few quiet moments each morning thanking the Giver. When we begin each day with heads bowed and hearts lifted, we remind ourselves of God's love, His protection, and His commandments. And if we are wise, we align our priorities for the coming day with the teachings and commandments that God has given us through His Holy Word.

The path to spiritual maturity unfolds day by day. Each day offers the opportunity to worship God, to ignore God, or to rebel against God. When we worship Him with our prayers, our words, our thoughts, and our actions, we are blessed by the richness of our relationship with the Father. But if we ignore God altogether or intentionally rebel against His commandments, we rob ourselves of His blessings.

Today offers yet another opportunity for spiritual growth. If you choose, you can seize that opportunity by obeying God's Word, by seeking His will, and by walking with His Son.

Are you seeking to change some aspect of your life? Do you seek to improve the condition of your spiritual, physical, emotional, or financial health? If so, ask for God's help and ask for it many times each day . . . starting with your morning devotional.

A child of God should never leave his bedroom in
the morning without being on good terms with God.

C. H. SPURGEON

The moment you wake up each morning,
all your wishes and hopes for the day rush at you
like wild animals. And the first job each morning
consists in shoving it all back; in listening to that
other voice, taking that other point of view,
letting that other, larger, stronger,
quieter life coming flowing in.

C. S. LEWIS

Surrender your mind to the Lord
at the beginning of each day.

WARREN WIERSBE

How motivating it has been for me to view my early
morning devotions as a time of retreat alone with
Jesus, who desires that I "come with Him by myself
to a quiet place" in order to pray, read His Word,
listen for His voice, and be renewed in my spirit.

ANNE GRAHAM LOTZ

MORE FROM GOD'S WORD

*It is good to praise the LORD and make music to
your name, O Most High, to proclaim your love
in the morning and your faithfulness at night . . . .*

PSALM 92:1-2 NIV

*But I will sing of your strength, in the morning
I will sing of your love; for you are my fortress,
my refuge in times of trouble.*

PSALM 59:16 NIV

TODAY, I WILL THINK ABOUT . . .

The importance of starting each day
with a time of prayer, meditation, and Bible study.

A PRAYER TO START MY DAY

Dear Lord, help me to hear Your direction for my
life in the solitary moments that I spend with You.
And as I fulfill my responsibilities throughout
the day, let my actions and my thoughts
be pleasing to You. —Amen

DAY 26

WHOM WILL YOU SERVE TODAY?

WHOEVER WANTS TO BECOME GREAT
AMONG YOU MUST BE YOUR SERVANT,
AND WHOEVER WANTS TO BE FIRST
AMONG YOU MUST BE YOUR SLAVE;
JUST AS THE SON OF MAN DID NOT COME
TO BE SERVED, BUT TO SERVE,
AND TO GIVE HIS LIFE—A RANSOM FOR MANY.

MATTHEW 20:26-28 HCSB

Jesus teaches that the most esteemed men and women are not the leaders of society or the captains of industry. To the contrary, Jesus teaches that the greatest among us are those who choose to minister and to serve.

Today, you may feel the temptation to build yourself up in the eyes of your neighbors. Resist that temptation. Instead, serve your neighbors quietly and without fanfare. Find a need and fill it . . . humbly. Lend a helping hand and share a word of kindness . . . anonymously.

As you plan for the upcoming day, make plans to minister to those in need. Then, when you have done your best to serve your neighbors and to serve your God, you can rest comfortably knowing that in the eyes of God you have achieved greatness. And God's eyes, after all, are the only ones that really count.

If the attitude of servanthood is learned,
by attending to God as Lord, then, serving others
will develop as a very natural way of life.

EUGENE PETERSON

There are times when we are called to love,
expecting nothing in return. There are times when
we are called to give money to people who will
never say thanks, to forgive those who
won't forgive us, to come early and stay late
when no one else notices.

MAX LUCADO

Carve your name on hearts, not on marble.

C. H. SPURGEON

Do things for others and you'll find
your self-consciousness evaporating like
morning dew on a Missouri cornfield in July.

DALE CARNEGIE

MORE FROM GOD'S WORD

*Then a Samaritan traveling down the road came to
where the hurt man was. When he saw the man,
he felt very sorry for him. The Samaritan went to him,
poured olive oil and wine on his wounds,
and bandaged them. Then he put the hurt man
on his own donkey and took him to an inn
where he cared for him.*

LUKE 10:33-34 NCV

TODAY, I WILL THINK ABOUT . . .

Creative ways that I can serve others.

A PRAYER TO START MY DAY

Dear Lord, give me a servant's heart.
When Jesus humbled Himself and became a servant,
He also became an example for His followers.
Make me a faithful steward of my gifts, and let me
share with those in need. —Amen

THE PATH TO SPIRITUAL GROWTH

GROW IN GRACE AND UNDERSTANDING
OF OUR MASTER AND SAVIOR, JESUS CHRIST.
GLORY TO THE MASTER,
NOW AND FOREVER! YES!

2 PETER 3:18 MSG

The journey toward spiritual maturity lasts a lifetime: As Christians, we can and should continue to grow in the love and the knowledge of our Savior as long as we live. Norman Vincent Peale had simple advice for believers of all ages: "Ask the God who made you to keep remaking you." That advice, of course, is perfectly sound, but too often ignored.

When we cease to grow, either emotionally or spiritually, we do ourselves and our families a profound disservice. But, if we study God's Word, if we obey His commandments, and if we live in the center of His will, we will not be stagnant believers; we will, instead, be growing Christians . . . and that's exactly what God wants for our lives.

In those quiet moments when we open our hearts to God, the Creator who made us keeps remaking us. He gives us direction, perspective, wisdom, and courage. And, the appropriate moment to accept His spiritual gifts is always this one.

Some people have received Christ but have never reached spiritual maturity. We should grow as Christians every day, and we are not completely mature until we live in the presence of Christ.

BILLY GRAHAM

Each moment of our existence,
we are either growing into more or
retreating into less.

BRENNAN MANNING

Grass that is here today and gone tomorrow
does not require much time to mature.
A big oak tree that lasts for generations requires
much more time to grow and mature.
God is concerned about your life through eternity.
Allow Him to take all the time He needs
to shape you for His purposes. Larger assignments
will require longer periods of preparation.

HENRY BLACKABY

When you're through changing, you're through!

JOHN MAXWELL

MORE FROM GOD'S WORD

*Long for the pure milk of the word,
so that by it you may grow in respect to salvation.*

1 PETER 2:2 NASB

*Know the love of Christ which surpasses knowledge,
that you may be filled up to all the fullness of God.*

EPHESIANS 3:19 NASB

TODAY, I WILL THINK ABOUT . . .

The importance of continuing to grow
in the knowledge and love of the Lord.

A PRAYER TO START MY DAY

Lord, help me to keep growing
spiritually and emotionally. Let me live
according to Your Word, and let me grow
in my faith every day that I live. —Amen

DAY 28

TAKING TIME TO GIVE THANKS

ENTER INTO HIS GATES WITH THANKSGIVING,
AND INTO HIS COURTS WITH PRAISE.
BE THANKFUL TO HIM, AND BLESS
HIS NAME. FOR THE LORD IS GOOD;
HIS MERCY IS EVERLASTING, AND HIS TRUTH
ENDURES TO ALL GENERATIONS.

PSALM 100:4-5 NKJV

As believing Christians, we are blessed beyond measure. God sent His only Son to die for our sins. And, God has given us the priceless gifts of eternal love and eternal life. We, in turn, are instructed to approach our Heavenly Father with reverence and thanksgiving. But sometimes, in the crush of everyday living, we simply don't stop long enough to pause and thank our Creator for the countless blessings He has bestowed upon us.

When we slow down and express our gratitude to the One who made us, we enrich our own lives and the lives of those around us. Thanksgiving should become a habit, a regular part of our daily routines. God has blessed us beyond measure, and we owe Him everything, including our eternal praise.

So, as you plan for the day ahead, make plans to thank God for all His blessings. You owe your Heavenly Father everything, including your eternal praise . . . starting right now.

A Christian who walks by faith accepts all circumstances from God. He thanks God when everything goes good, when everything goes bad, and for the "blues" somewhere in between. He thanks God whether he feels like it or not.

ERWIN LUTZER

When it comes to life, the critical thing is whether you take things for granted or take them with gratitude.

G. K. CHESTERTON

One act of thanksgiving when things go wrong with us is worth a thousand thanks when things are agreeable to our inclination.

JOHN OF AVILA

The devil moves in when a Christian starts to complain, but thanksgiving in the Spirit defeats the devil and glorifies the Lord.

WARREN WIERSBE

MORE FROM GOD'S WORD

Thanks be to God for His indescribable gift.

2 CORINTHIANS 9:15 HCSB

Let the peace of Christ rule in your hearts,
since as members of one body you were called to peace.
And be thankful.

COLOSSIANS 3:15 NIV

TODAY, I WILL THINK ABOUT . . .

The urgent need to thank God for His gifts.

A PRAYER TO START MY DAY

Dear Lord, You have given me so many blessings,
and You want to give me even more.
Thank You. Here's how I will show my thanks:
I will have a good attitude, I will be kind to
other people, and I will behave myself. —Amen

RECEIVING GOD'S ABUNDANCE

I HAVE COME THAT THEY MAY HAVE LIFE,
AND THAT THEY MAY HAVE IT
MORE ABUNDANTLY.

JOHN 10:10 NKJV

God does not promise us abundance. He promises that we "may have life" and that we "may have it more abundantly" *if* we accept His grace, His blessings, and His Son (John 10:10 NKJV). When we commit our hearts and our days to the One who created us, we experience spiritual abundance through the grace and sacrifice of His Son, Jesus. But, when we focus our thoughts and energies, not upon God's perfect will for our lives, but instead upon our own unending assortments of earthly needs and desires, we inevitably forfeit the spiritual abundance that might otherwise be ours.

Today and every day, seek God's will for your life and follow it. Today, turn your worries and your concerns over to your Heavenly Father. Today, seek God's wisdom, follow His commandments, trust His judgment, and honor His Son. When you do, spiritual abundance will be yours, not just for this day, but for all eternity.

Instead of living a black-and-white existence,
we'll be released into a Technicolor world
of vibrancy and emotion when we more accurately
reflect His nature to the world around us.

BILL HYBELS

The only way you can experience abundant life
is to surrender your plans to Him.

CHARLES STANLEY

People, places, and things were
never meant to give us life.
God alone is the author of a fulfilling life.

GARY SMALLEY & JOHN TRENT

Jesus wants Life for us, Life with a capital L.

JOHN ELDREDGE

The man who lives without Jesus is
the poorest of the poor, whereas no one is so rich as
the man who lives in His grace.

THOMAS À KEMPIS

MORE FROM GOD'S WORD

And God will generously provide all you need.
Then you will always have everything you need and
plenty left over to share with others.

2 CORINTHIANS 9:8 NLT

The master was full of praise.
"Well done, my good and faithful servant.
You have been faithful in handling this small amount,
so now I will give you many more responsibilities.
Let's celebrate together!"

MATTHEW 25:21 NLT

TODAY, I WILL THINK ABOUT . . .

The spiritual abundance that can be mine in Christ.

A PRAYER TO START MY DAY

Dear Lord, You have offered me the gift of
abundance through Your Son. Thank You, Father,
for the abundant life that is mine through
Christ Jesus. Let me accept His gifts and
use them always to glorify You. —Amen

ACCEPTING GOD'S GIFT

FOR GOD SO LOVED THE WORLD THAT
HE GAVE HIS ONLY BEGOTTEN SON,
THAT WHOEVER BELIEVES IN HIM SHOULD
NOT PERISH BUT HAVE EVERLASTING LIFE.

JOHN 3:16 NKJV

How marvelous it is that God became a man and walked among us. Had He not chosen to do so, we might feel removed from a distant Creator. But ours is not a distant God. Ours is a God who understands—far better than we ever could—the essence of what it means to be human.

God understands our hopes, our fears, and our temptations. He understands what it means to be angry and what it costs to forgive. He knows the heart, the conscience, and the soul of every person who has ever lived, including you. And God has a plan of salvation that is intended for you. Accept it. Accept God's gift through the person of His Son Christ Jesus, and then rest assured: God walked among us so that you might have eternal life; amazing though it may seem, He did it for you.

Salvation involves so much more than
knowing facts about Jesus Christ, or even
having special feelings toward Jesus Christ.
Salvation comes to us when, by an act of will,
we receive Christ as our Savior and Lord.

WARREN WIERSBE

When I read that Christ Jesus came into the world
to save sinners, it was as if day suddenly broke
on a dark night.

THOMAS BILNEY

Salvation is a personal matter.
Nobody will die for you, and nobody will stand
in your place at the judgment bar of God.

SAM JONES

The saving of men from sin is the biggest enterprise
on earth, for it was the only cause
big enough to bring the Son of God
from heaven to die on the cross.

R. G. LEE

MORE FROM GOD'S WORD

But God demonstrates his own love for us in this:
While we were still sinners, Christ died for us.

ROMANS 5:8 NIV

If you confess with your mouth, "Jesus is Lord,"
and believe in your heart that God raised Him from
the dead, you will be saved. With the heart one believes,
resulting in righteousness, and with the mouth
one confesses, resulting in salvation.

ROMANS 10:9-10 HCSB

TODAY, I WILL THINK ABOUT . . .

Christ's sacrifice for me . . . and God's love for me.

A PRAYER TO START MY DAY

Lord, I'm only here on earth for a brief visit.
Heaven is my real home. You've given me
the gift of eternal life through Your Son Jesus.
I accept Your gift, Lord. And I'll share
Your Good News so that others, too, might come
to know Christ's healing touch. —Amen

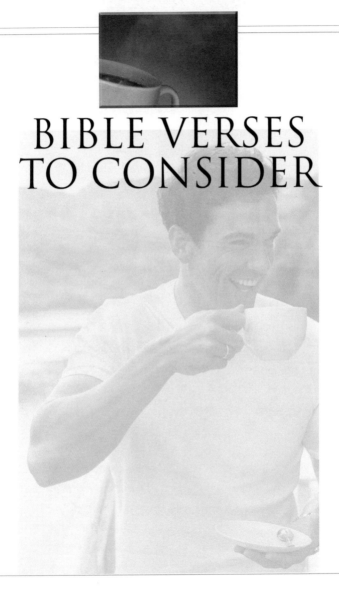

BIBLE VERSES
TO CONSIDER

HOLINESS

But now you must be holy in everything you do,
just as God—who chose you to be his children—is holy.
For he himself has said,
"You must be holy because I am holy."

1 PETER 1:15-16 NLT

But Daniel purposed in his heart that
he would not defile himself . . . .

DANIEL 1:8 KJV

Therefore come out from them and be separate,
says the Lord. Touch no unclean thing,
and I will receive you.

2 CORINTHIANS 6:17 NIV

No discipline seems pleasant at the time, but painful.
Later on, however, it produces a harvest of righteousness
and peace for those who have been trained by it.

HEBREWS 12:11 NIV

YOU WILL TEACH ME HOW TO LIVE
A HOLY LIFE. BEING WITH YOU
WILL FILL ME WITH JOY;
AT YOUR RIGHT HAND I WILL FIND
PLEASURE FOREVER.

—

PSALM 16:11 NCV

JOY

A joyful heart is good medicine, but a broken spirit dries up the bones.

PROVERBS 17:22 NASB

Rejoice in the Lord always. I will say it again: Rejoice!

PHILIPPIANS 4:4 HCSB

I will thank you, LORD, with all my heart;
I will tell of all the marvelous things you have done.
I will be filled with joy because of you.
I will sing praises to your name, O Most High.

PSALM 9:1-2 NLT

May the God of hope fill you with all joy and
peace as you trust in him, so that you may overflow
with hope by the power of the Holy Spirit.

ROMANS 15:13 NIV

WEEPING MAY ENDURE
FOR A NIGHT,
BUT JOY COMES IN THE MORNING.

———

PSALM 30:5 NKJV

MISSIONS

Now then we are ambassadors for Christ . . . .

2 CORINTHIANS 5:20 KJV

*After these things the Lord appointed other seventy also,
and sent them two and two before his face into every city
and place, whither he himself would come. Therefore
said he unto them, The harvest truly is great, but
the laborers are few: pray ye therefore the Lord
of the harvest, that he would send forth laborers
into his harvest. Go your ways: behold,
I send you forth as lambs among wolves.*

LUKE 10:1-3 KJV

*Then Jesus came to them and said, "All authority
in heaven and on earth has been given to me.
Therefore go and make disciples of all nations,
baptizing them in the name of the Father and of
the Son and of the Holy Spirit, and teaching them to
obey everything I have commanded you. And surely
I am with you always, to the very end of the age."*

MATTHEW 28:18-20 NIV

I WILL ALSO MAKE YOU
A LIGHT OF THE NATIONS
SO THAT MY SALVATION
MAY REACH TO THE END
OF THE EARTH.

—

ISAIAH 49:6 NASB

RENEWAL

. . . inwardly we are being renewed day by day.

2 CORINTHIANS 4:16 NIV

*I will give you a new heart and put
a new spirit in you . . . .*

EZEKIEL 36:26 NIV

*Do you not know? Have you not heard?
The Everlasting God, the LORD, the Creator of
the ends of the earth does not become weary or tired.
His understanding is inscrutable. He gives strength to
the weary, and to him who lacks might He
increases power. Though youths grow weary and tired,
and vigorous young men stumble badly, yet those who
wait for the LORD will gain new strength; they will
mount up with wings like eagles, they will run and not
get tired, they will walk and not become weary.*

ISAIAH 40:28-31 NASB

*"For I will restore health to you and heal you
of your wounds," says the LORD.*

JEREMIAH 30:17 NKJV

THEREFORE IF ANYONE
IS IN CHRIST,
HE IS A NEW CREATURE;
THE OLD THINGS PASSED AWAY;
BEHOLD,
NEW THINGS HAVE COME.

—

2 CORINTHIANS 5:17 HCSB

HONESTY

So put away all falsehood and "tell your neighbor the truth" because we belong to each other.

EPHESIANS 4:25 NLT

The honest person will live in safety, but the dishonest will be caught.

PROVERBS 10:9 NCV

The LORD abhors dishonest scales . . . .

PROVERBS 11:1 NIV

You've gotten a reputation as a bad-news people, you people of Judah and Israel, but I'm coming to save you. From now on, you're the good-news people. Don't be afraid. Keep a firm grip on what I'm doing.

ZECHARIAH 8:13 MSG

THE GODLY ARE DIRECTED
BY THEIR HONESTY.

—

PROVERBS 11:5 NLT

MISTAKES

If we confess our sins to him,
he is faithful and just to forgive us and
to cleanse us from every wrong.

1 JOHN 1:9 NLT

You were taught, with regard to your former way of life,
to put off your old self, which is being corrupted
by its deceitful desires; to be made new in the attitude
of your minds; and to put on the new self,
created to be like God in true righteousness and holiness.

EPHESIANS 4:22-24 NIV

Have mercy on me, O God, according to
your unfailing love; according to your great compassion
blot out my transgressions. Wash away all
my iniquity and cleanse me from my sin.

PSALM 51:1-2 NIV

IF YOU LISTEN TO
CONSTRUCTIVE CRITICISM,
YOU WILL BE AT HOME
AMONG THE WISE.

—

PROVERBS 15:31 NLT

REPENTANCE

I preached that they should repent and turn to God and prove their repentance by their deeds.

ACTS 26:20 NIV

You were taught to leave your old self—to stop living the evil way you lived before. That old self becomes worse, because people are fooled by the evil things they want to do. But you were taught to be made new in your hearts, to become a new person. That new person is made to be like God—made to be truly good and holy.

EPHESIANS 4:22-24 NCV

But their scribes and Pharisees murmured against his disciples, saying, Why do ye eat and drink with publicans and sinners? And Jesus answering said unto them, They that are whole need not a physician; but they that are sick. I came not to call the righteous, but sinners to repentance.

LUKE 5:30-32 KJV

The sacrifices of God are a broken spirit; a broken and contrite heart, O God, you will not despise.

PSALM 51:17 NIV

THEREFORE THIS IS WHAT
THE LORD SAYS:
"IF YOU REPENT,
I WILL RESTORE YOU
THAT YOU MAY SERVE ME . . . ."

—

JEREMIAH 15:19 NIV

JUDGING OTHERS

The LORD does not look at the things man looks at. Man looks at the outward appearance, but the LORD looks at the heart.

1 SAMUEL 16:7 NIV

Speak and act as those who will be judged by the law of freedom. For judgment is without mercy to the one who hasn't shown mercy. Mercy triumphs over judgment.

JAMES 2:12-13 HCSB

Why do you look at the speck of sawdust in your brother's eye and pay no attention to the plank in your own eye? How can you say to your brother, "Let me take the speck out of your eye," when all the time there is a plank in your own eye? You hypocrite, first take the plank out of your own eye, and then you will see clearly to remove the speck from your brother's eye.

MATTHEW 7:3-5 NIV

You, therefore, have no excuse, you who pass judgment on someone else, for at whatever point you judge the other, you are condemning yourself.

ROMANS 2:1 NIV

DO NOT JUDGE,
AND YOU WILL NOT BE JUDGED.
DO NOT CONDEMN, AND YOU WILL
NOT BE CONDEMNED. FORGIVE,
AND YOU WILL BE FORGIVEN.

—

LUKE 6:37 HCSB

HOPE

*Let us hold on to the confession of our hope
without wavering, for He who promised is faithful.*

HEBREWS 10:23 HCSB

*This hope we have as an anchor of the soul,
a hope both sure and steadfast.*

HEBREWS 6:19 NASB

Happy is he . . . whose hope is in the LORD his God.

PSALM 146:5 KJV

I find rest in God; only he gives me hope.

PSALM 62:5 NCV

*You are my hope; O Lord GOD,
You are my confidence.*

PSALM 71:5 NASB

OPTIMISM

I can do everything through him that gives me strength.

PHILIPPIANS 4:13 NIV

*My cup runs over. Surely goodness and
mercy shall follow me all the days of my life;
and I will dwell in the house of the LORD Forever.*

PSALM 23:5-6 NKJV

*The LORD is my light and my salvation;
whom shall I fear?
The LORD is the strength of my life;
of whom shall I be afraid?*

PSALM 27:1 KJV

*But we are hoping for something we do not have yet,
and we are waiting for it patiently.*

ROMANS 8:25 NCV

Make me hear joy and gladness.

PSALM 51:8 NKJV

SEEKING GOD

But if from there you seek the LORD your God,
you will find him if you look for him with
all your heart and with all your soul.

DEUTERONOMY 4:29 NIV

Seek the LORD while he may be found;
call on him while he is near.

ISAIAH 55:6 NIV

This is what the LORD says to the house of Israel: "Seek
me and live."

AMOS 5:4 NIV

Ask and it will be given to you; seek and you will find;
knock and the door will be opened to you.
For everyone who asks receives; he who seeks finds;
and to him who knocks, the door will be opened.

MATTHEW 7:7-8 NIV

God did this so that men
would seek him and perhaps
reach out for him and
find him, though he is not far
from each one of us.

—

Acts 17:27 niv

KINDNESS

Finally, all of you should be of one mind,
full of sympathy toward each other,
loving one another with tender hearts and humble minds.

1 PETER 3:8 NLT

Be kind to one another, tender-hearted,
forgiving each other, just as God
in Christ also has forgiven you.

EPHESIANS 4:32 NASB

Don't ever forget kindness and truth.
Wear them like a necklace.
Write them on your heart as if on a tablet.

PROVERBS 3:3 NCV

May God, who gives this patience and encouragement,
help you live in complete harmony with each other—
each with the attitude of Christ Jesus toward the other.

ROMANS 15:5 NLT

I TELL YOU THE TRUTH,
ANYTHING YOU DID FOR EVEN
THE LEAST OF MY PEOPLE HERE,
YOU ALSO DID FOR ME.

—

MATTHEW 25:40 NCV

PATIENCE

Always be humble, gentle, and patient,
accepting each other in love.

EPHESIANS 4:2 NCV

Yet the LORD longs to be gracious to you;
he rises to show you compassion.
For the LORD is a God of justice.
Blessed are all who wait for him!

ISAIAH 30:18 NIV

The LORD is wonderfully good to those who
wait for him and seek him.
So it is good to wait quietly for salvation from the LORD.

LAMENTATIONS 3:25-26 NLT

Wait on the LORD; Be of good courage,
and He shall strengthen your heart;
Wait, I say, on the LORD!

PSALM 27:14 NKJV

PATIENCE IS BETTER THAN
STRENGTH.

PROVERBS 16:32 NCV

PRAISE

Is anyone happy? Let him sing songs of praise.

JAMES 5:13 NIV

*Enter into His gates with thanksgiving,
and into His courts with praise. Be thankful to Him,
and bless His name. For the LORD is good;
His mercy is everlasting, and His truth endures
to all generations.*

PSALM 100:4-5 NKJV

*Praise the LORD! Oh, give thanks to the LORD,
for He is good! For His mercy endures forever.*

PSALM 106:1 NKJV

*Praise God, everybody! Applaud God, all people!
His love has taken over our lives;
God's faithful ways are eternal. Hallelujah!*

PSALM 117:1-2 MSG

I WILL PRAISE THE LORD
AT ALL TIMES, I WILL CONSTANTLY
SPEAK HIS PRAISES.

———

PSALM 34:1 NLT

INTEGRITY

Till I die, I will not deny my integrity.
I will maintain my righteousness and never let go of it;
my conscience will not reproach me as long as I live.

JOB 27:5-6 NIV

People with integrity have firm footing,
but those who follow crooked paths will slip and fall.

PROVERBS 10:9 NLT

The godly walk with integrity;
blessed are their children after them.

PROVERBS 20:7 NLT

Innocent people will be kept safe,
but those who are dishonest will suddenly be ruined.

PROVERBS 28:18 NCV